Astronaut

Peggy J. Parks

KIDHAVEN PRESS
An imprint of Thomson Gale, a part of The Thomson Corporation

THOMSON
—————✦————— ™
GALE

Detroit • New York • San Francisco • San Diego
New Haven, Conn.• Waterville, Maine • London • Munich

THOMSON

─────────✦─────────™

GALE

For more information, contact
KidHaven Press
27500 Drake Rd.
Farmington Hills, MI 48331-3535
Or you can visit our Internet site at http://www.gale.com

LIBRARY OF CONGRESS CATALOGING-IN-PUBLICATION DATA

Parks, Peggy J., 1951–
  Astronaut / by Peggy J. Parks.
    p. cm. — (Exploring careers)
  Includes bibliographical references and index.
  ISBN 0-7377-3016-1 (hard cover : alk. paper) 1. Astronautics—Vocational guid-ance—Juvenile literature. 2. Astronauts—Juvenile literature. 3. Astronauts—Training of—Juvenile literature.' I. Title. II. Exploring careers (KidHaven Press)
  TL850.P37 2005
  629.45'0023—dc22
 	
                                                                                    2005017247

Printed in the United States of America

CONTENTS

CHAPTER 1

Star Sailors

"It's hard to explain how amazing and magical this experience is. . . . There's the astounding beauty and diversity of the planet itself, scrolling across your view at what appears to be a smooth, stately pace. Actually, it's zooming past at about 18,000 miles an hour, but there's no sound or wind to convince you of this."[1] Astronaut Kathryn Sullivan wrote these words about the journeys she has made into space. She and her fellow astronauts are people whose careers are devoted to space exploration. Their very title describes them—the word *astronaut* comes from Greek words meaning "star sailor."

Astronauts throughout the world work for different space organizations. For example, Russian astronauts, called **cosmonauts**, work for the Russian Space Agency. Astronauts from countries in Europe work for the European Space Agency. U. S. astronauts work for the National Aeronautics and Space Administration, more commonly known as NASA.

Astronauts devote their careers to space exploration.

Early Spacecraft

Astronauts who traveled on early space missions flew in spacecraft that were used only once. Powerful rockets propelled them off the launchpad and away from the strong pull of Earth's gravity. Once the spacecraft had climbed far enough, its big rockets dropped off. The spacecraft continued on

Space shuttles are spacecraft that look like large, high-tech airplanes.

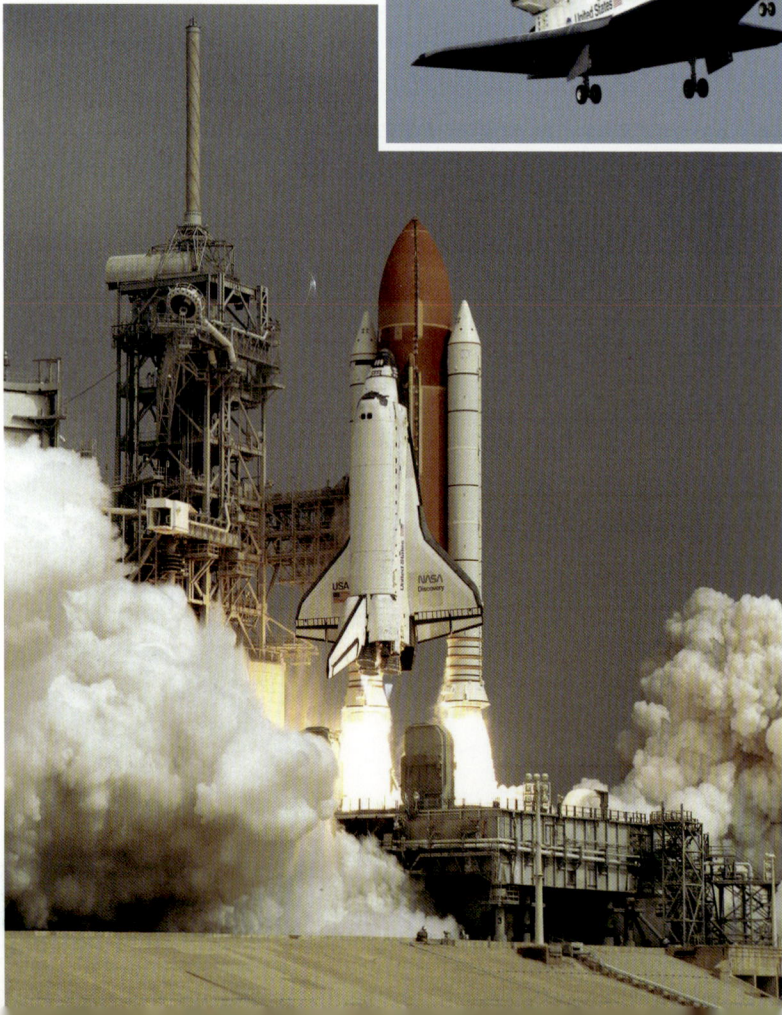

its way, with smaller rockets providing power when needed. When the mission was over, the astronauts headed back toward Earth. As the spacecraft got closer, huge parachutes opened to slow it down. It splashed into the ocean, where rescue crews were waiting with rubber rafts. The astronauts climbed out of the spacecraft and into the rafts. Then a helicopter lifted them out of the rafts. The spacecraft was hauled away to be displayed at NASA or in a space museum.

Spacecraft Today

Astronauts no longer have to be fished out of the ocean after a space mission. Instead, they travel on **space shuttles**. These are nothing like spacecraft of the past because they are reusable. Space shuttles look like big, high-tech airplanes. They are attached to **booster rockets** that blast them off the launchpad. The shuttles travel so fast that it takes them just eight and half minutes to reach orbit. About two minutes after lift off, the boosters drop off and return to Earth by parachute. Engines keep the shuttle moving until it reaches its orbit. Then the engines shut off and the spacecraft coasts along like a glider. When the mission is over, the shuttle flies back to Earth. It has landing gear similar to a jet airplane, but its landing speed is much faster than a jet. To help bring it to a stop, an enormous parachute (known as a drag chute) pops out of the back. Once the astronauts are out of the spacecraft, maintenance crews take it away. They spend thousands of hours making repairs and getting the shuttle ready for the next mission.

Flying the Spacecraft

The crew of a space shuttle is made up of three types of astronauts: a **commander**, a **pilot**, and several **mission specialists**. A commander is the astronaut in charge of the mission. Commanders have a great deal of responsibility because the success or failure of the mission rests on their shoulders. They give orders and make decisions. Commanders are ultimately responsible for the spacecraft and the safety of the crew.

Pilots are second in command on space flights. It is the pilot's job to assist the commander with controlling and operating the spacecraft. Pilot astronauts who gain enough experience and skills may eventually become commanders. Eileen Collins is an astronaut commander. In 1995, she became the first woman to pilot a space shuttle. She flew the *Discovery* more than 200 miles into space to reach Mir, a Russian space station. Collins flew the shuttle around Mir as a test. During the next mission to Mir, the space shuttle would **dock** with the space station. Two years later, Collins piloted another space shuttle called *Atlantis*. Once again she flew to Mir, and this time she docked with it. The shuttle crew delivered water and other supplies to the astronauts staying at Mir.

In 1999 Collins became NASA's first female commander. She was in charge of a mission on the space shuttle *Columbia*. The goal involved launching an instrument called the Chandra X-ray Observatory. Once it was in orbit, it used X-ray technology to study space phenomena such as exploding stars and black holes.

Collin's most recent mission was in July 2005, when she commanded the space shuttle *Discovery*. It was the first U.S. space flight since the *Columbia* broke apart on February 1, 2003, killing all seven astronauts aboard.

Science Experts

Each shuttle mission has a crew of five to seven astronauts. Mission specialists are part of these crews.

Eileen Collins, NASA's first female commander, enters notes in a log during the 1999 *Columbia* mission.

They are usually scientists or engineers. Each mission specialist is responsible for a certain part of a mission, such as operating a specific piece of shuttle equipment. They perform space walks, scientific experiments, and research projects, as well as maintaining the shuttle's computer systems.

Sometimes mission specialists perform duties outside the spacecraft. In 1990, for instance, mission specialists Steven Hawley and Kathryn Sullivan launched the **Hubble Space Telescope**. This is a huge observatory that is constantly in orbit nearly 400 miles (644km) in space. The Hubble is fitted with sophisticated cameras and other instruments that help scientists study the universe.

Mission specialists consult a chart during a space shuttle flight. Mission specialists perform a variety of tasks during space missions.

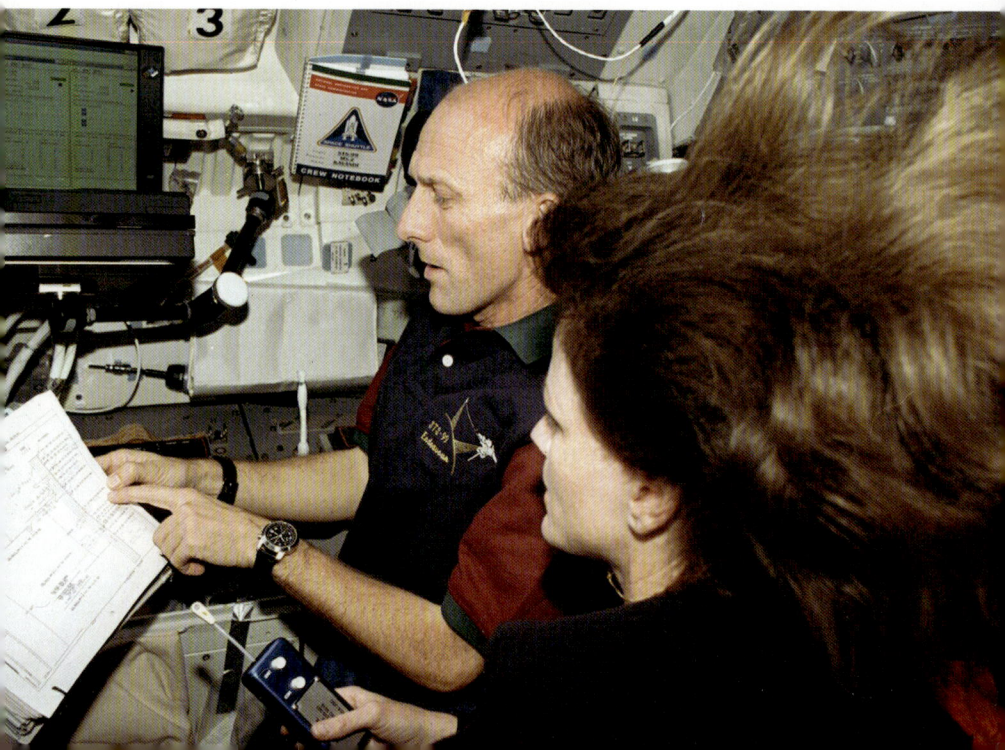

The World's Largest Space Laboratory

The **International Space Station** (ISS) is also in permanent orbit around the Earth. This spacecraft, however, is designed to be a place where astronauts can live and work. The ISS floats in space, orbiting the Earth once every 90 minutes. Construction began in 1998 and is expected to be completed in the next few years. Sixteen nations are helping with the project, including the United States, Canada, Russia, Japan, and a number of countries in Europe. The ISS is being assembled one section at a time, and the process has been compared to making a building out of Legos—but this structure will be enormous. When the space station is complete, it will weigh more than a million pounds (454 metric tons). It will be the world's largest space laboratory. Inside, it will be roomy enough to comfortably house seven astronauts.

One important role of the ISS is to help astronauts get used to spending long periods of time in space. This will prepare them for future missions, such as trips to Mars. When the day comes for astronauts to visit Mars, they will be away from Earth for a year or more. Such long space visits will present many challenges that humans have never faced. Living in the ISS will help astronauts learn how to cope with such challenges.

Space exploration has changed greatly over the years. The spacecraft of yesterday have been replaced with high-tech shuttles that can fly into space, return

Astronauts relax inside the International Space Station (top). A computer-generated image of the ISS (bottom) shows an exterior view of the station in June 2005.

to Earth, and land like an airplane. An orbiting space station provides astronauts with a scientific laboratory in the sky. The astronauts on these missions may be commanders, pilots, or mission specialists. But they all share one thing in common: a fascination with space and all its mysteries.

CHAPTER 2

What It Takes to Be an Astronaut

Most astronauts say they dreamed of visiting space from the time they were children. They were intrigued by early space programs such as Mercury and Gemini, and the Apollo flights to the Moon. Some decided at a young age to become astronauts, while others made the decision later in life. But no matter how they arrived at where they are today, astronauts are people who love their jobs. Yet they are the first to say that becoming an astronaut is far from easy. Even after years of education and special training, only the best of the best ever make it.

Early Preparation

People who are interested in becoming astronauts must go to college and earn a bachelor's degree.

Students listen during a college lecture. People interested in becoming astronauts must complete college.

However, NASA advises students to start preparing when they are young. Aspiring astronauts should take every science and math class that is offered in school. Eileen Collins often talks to young people who say they do not like math because it is too hard, and she offers some advice: "It's the kind of thing that if you work at it long enough, you're going to get it, and once you get it, you find that you have a love for it. Math is almost like music . . . it's not really just a science, it's an art."[2]

Math and science are important subjects because of NASA's selection requirements. When reviewing applications for its astronaut program, the agency looks carefully at what people studied in college. Those with degrees in areas such as biological or physical science, astronomy, chemistry, engineering, or mathematics have the best chance of being accepted.

Work Experience

Along with a college degree, applicants must also have work experience in their chosen field. For instance, pilot astronauts must accumulate at least 1,000 hours of flight time piloting a jet aircraft. NASA prefers those who have also worked as test pilots, flying experimental airplanes for the U.S. Air Force, Navy, or Marine Corps. Astronaut Pam Melroy is a former test pilot. She started as an air force pilot who

Astronaut Pam Melroy was a test pilot for the air force before NASA selected her as an astronaut candidate.

flew combat missions over Iraq and Saudi Arabia in the Gulf War. Then she was accepted in the air force's elite Test Pilot School. She describes that training as "kind of like getting a master's degree in flying at the same time you're getting a master's degree in aeronautical engineering."[3]

Work experience is also required for people who want to be mission specialists. After earning their degree, applicants must work for at least three years in a job that is related to their field of study. Joe Acaba, who is a mission specialist–educator, worked as a hydrogeologist, or a scientist who studies water under the ground. Before becoming an astronaut, Acaba worked for five years as a middle school math and science teacher.

Advanced Degrees

NASA does not require work experience for applicants who have advanced college degrees—and nearly all astronauts do. Many have earned master's degrees or PhDs in areas such as earth science, physics, aeronautics, engineering, and mathematics. Astronaut Megan McArthur earned her PhD in oceanography. She knew her chances of becoming an astronaut were slim, so she decided to become an oceanographer, or a scientist who studies ocean life. Yet she never stopped thinking about joining NASA, as she explains: "I decided to pursue oceanography because I thought it was such an exciting field . . . but always in the back of my mind there was this idea that someday maybe

I would still become an astronaut."[4]

The Selection Process

Despite the tough competition, McArthur applied to NASA. A full year later, she got a phone call saying she had been accepted in NASA's astronaut training program. After receiving the call, she says, she could not stop smiling for a week.

Joe Acaba worked as a math teacher before becoming a NASA mission specialist.

NASA receives thousands of applications each year from aspiring astronauts all over the world. Every two years, about a hundred applicants are invited to the Lyndon B. Johnson Space Center in Houston. Over the course of a week, they go through a tough screening process. First, they have extensive physical examinations. If they pass the physicals, they participate in a number of meetings. Applicants are evaluated by psychologists, interviewed by astronauts, and examined by the Astronaut Selection Board. When applicants are equally qualified, the final selection often depends on how well they present themselves in interviews. NASA looks for qualities such as excellent communication skills, enthusiasm, and a willingness to work as a team member. At the

end of the week, the applicants return home. The selection board chooses anywhere from ten to thirty of the best people to be the next "astronaut candidates."

Tough Training

For eighteen months to two years, the candidates participate in a tough and intense training program. They attend dozens of classes on astronomy, geology, meteorology, and other types of science and math. They learn about the space program, the ISS, and the space shuttles. They are trained to use navigation instruments, computer systems, electrical power, and engines. They also have training outside of the classroom. For instance, to get a real feel for space shuttles, the trainees climb inside a model known as a **simulator**. They lie on their backs and strap themselves in as if they are in a real vehicle heading toward space. Sometimes lights flash and sirens go off, and the future astronauts learn how to handle emergencies.

Another important part of the training is learning how to deal with weightlessness. In space, there is no gravity like there is on Earth. So astronauts are constantly floating. To learn how to cope with this, the candidates go up in a special airplane used for weightlessness training. McArthur says this is an interesting experience: "When you're weightless, there is nothing to stop you from scooting all over the place. At first, we were all grabbing onto each other with our arms and legs flailing. But when we got used to it, it was fun. We started showing off, curling up into balls, spinning each other around, and pretending we were flying like Superman!"[5]

Astronaut candidates also learn water survival training. This is necessary because if astronauts have to eject from an aircraft, they must be able to survive a water landing. Wearing bulky pressurized flight suits, trainees must open a parachute, land in the water, and then climb out of the parachute—even if it has wrapped them up like a cocoon! In addition, the trainees learn land survival techniques in case they are ever stranded on land.

Astronaut candidates participate in a training class. Candidates attend dozens of classes as part of their training.

As part of their training program, astronaut candidates experience weightlessness in the hull of a special aircraft in flight.

Full-Fledged Astronauts

When the candidates have finished training, they are given job assignments with NASA. How quickly they participate in a space mission depends on NASA's schedule. Most astronauts first visit space one to six years after they are fully trained.

Astronauts have jobs that are exciting and fascinating, but it is not easy to achieve what they have. It takes many years of education, special training, and hard work to make it. Young people who dream of becoming astronauts must be willing to do what it takes to succeed—and Melroy is one astronaut who hopes they will: "There's a child out there in school right now who will be the first person on Mars. It's extremely important to realize that this will happen in your lifetime, and you can play a part in this exciting adventure."[6]

CHAPTER 3

Astronauts at Work

No two astronauts do exactly the same thing from day to day. Their work varies based on their specialties and the projects to which they are assigned. Many of them work together to prepare for upcoming space flights. The mission crews are selected one to two years in advance. After astronauts are chosen for a mission, they must train and prepare for it. Numerous other astronauts who are not assigned to the flight help the crew members get ready. These people all work together as a team—and teamwork is essential for all astronauts, no matter what their specialty or job may be. Tom Jones, who has been an astronaut since 1991, explains the importance of teamwork: "All share the work and pain of months—even years—of preparation for each flight; all share the satisfaction and pride in a mission done well. . . . Exceptional team-work is the minimum standard in spaceflight—it can literally be a matter of life and death."[7]

Mission Training

This sort of teamwork means the astronauts work closely together to carry out the mission goals. But teamwork also helps reduce the potential for error—and mistakes on a space flight could be deadly. That is why astronauts assigned to a mission spend so much time training for it before they leave the ground. In NASA training sessions, the astronauts learn how to handle life on a spacecraft. Every possible action they will perform in space is practiced

A mission specialist wears virtual reality goggles as he trains for an upcoming mission.

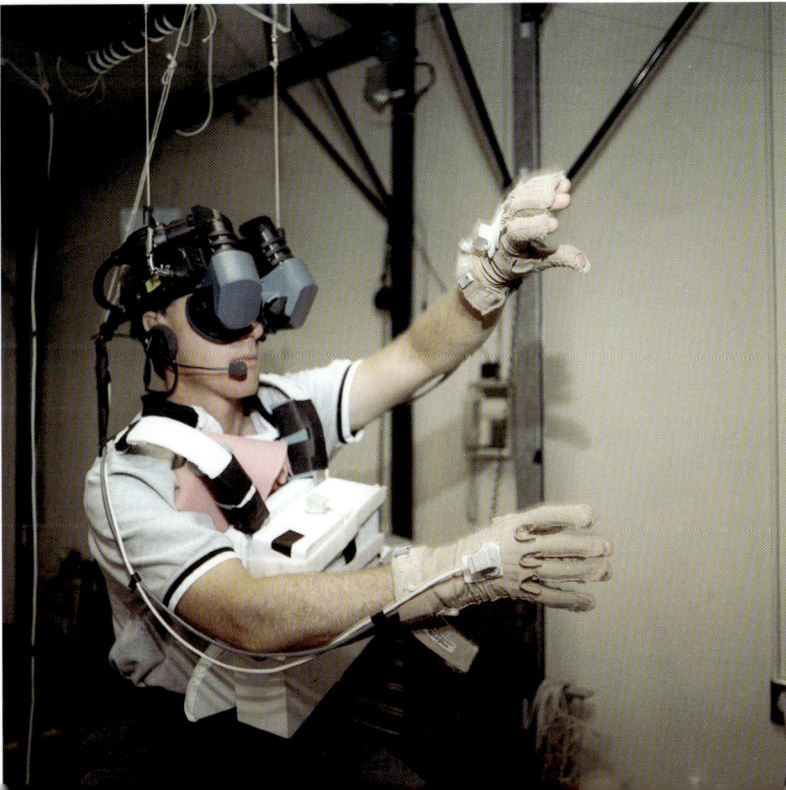

over and over again, from putting on a spacesuit to preparing meals. This repetition helps them perform their duties by instinct, almost without thinking about it. Constant practicing also teaches the astronauts how to react in crisis situations.

One method of training crew members is by using different types of simulators. For instance, the Neutral Buoyancy Laboratory prepares astronauts to perform a space walk. The facility has a large underwater tank that is 40 feet (12m) deep. It is the world's largest indoor pool—so large that a full-scale model of the space shuttle fits inside it! Astronauts train underwater because in water their bodies feel light, and they drift and float much the same as they do in space. Dressed in the same spacesuits and helmets they will wear during a space walk, the astronauts are submerged in the tank. There they can practice all experiments that they intend to perform on the space shuttle or ISS.

Another type of simulator helps pilots learn how to dock a space shuttle with the ISS. To train pilots in docking skills, NASA uses a video game console. Pilots use the video tool to practice making decisions and reacting quickly to emergencies.

The Real Thing

When the astronauts on a crew have finished preparing for a mission and have finally blasted off for space, it is the highlight of their career. This is where they can put all their skills, talents, and

In NASA's underwater Neutral Buoyancy Laboratory, an astronaut trains for a space walk.

training to work. The tasks the crew performs while they are in space depend on the mission and its goals. For instance, since the Hubble Space Telescope was launched, astronauts have kept it in working order. When it needs repairs, a space shuttle takes a crew to fix it.

One such mission was in December 1999, on the space shuttle *Discovery*. Mission specialists Steven Smith and John Grunsfeld went outside the shuttle to reach the Hubble. First, they hooked themselves to the telescope with safety tethers so they would not float off into space. Then they climbed up the enormous structure. Wearing bulky gloves to protect their hands, they used a tool called a socket wrench to unscrew tiny bolts. At one point, the socket popped off the wrench and began floating away

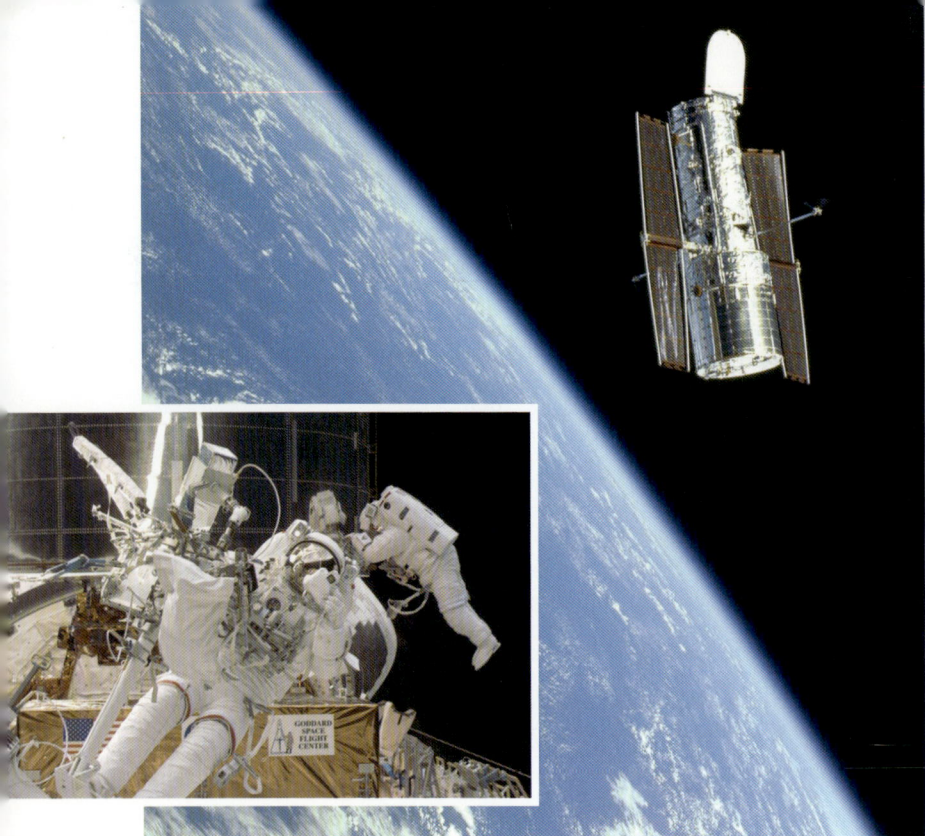

The Hubble Space Telescope floats above the Earth as astronauts Steven Smith and John Grunsfeld perform repairs on it in 1999 (inset).

Grunsfeld snatched it back, and he and Smith kept working. They replaced a failed radio transmitter and repaired some other scientific instruments. After working for more than eight hours on the repairs, the two astronauts returned to the shuttle. When the mission was finished, the crew returned to Earth.

Space Station Missions

Sometimes shuttles carry crews of astronauts to the ISS to deliver supplies or perform repairs. The shuttle commander must dock with the space station, which is a technique that absolutely must be precise. Even a small error could be disastrous, as NASA's Web site explains: "When you're guiding a 90,720-kilogram [200,000-pound] object moving at over 27,350 kilometers per hour [17,000 miles per hour] towards a seven-story structure . . . there is no room for miscalculation."[8]

Because it is such a risky endeavor, docking a space shuttle requires the efforts of the entire crew. As the commander slowly moves toward the ISS, the pilot reads off a checklist of actions to take and instruments to monitor. Mission specialists use a special laser gun to track the speed of the spacecraft. As the shuttle gets closer, the commander turns it around to approach the ISS tail-first. The shuttle slows down

A mission commander and pilot sit at their stations in the cockpit of a space shuttle.

even more, and the commander glides it into special docking grooves on the ISS. Once the shuttle and the ISS are docked together, they form one enormous spacecraft.

In July 2005, the space shuttle *Discovery* carried a crew of astronauts to the ISS. After commander Eileen Collins had the shuttle safely docked, the hatches opened and the crews from the two spacecraft greeted each other. The shuttle astronauts delivered supplies such as food, water, and clothing, as well as laptop computers, tools, and other equipment. Throughout the mission, astronauts could float freely back and forth between the two spacecraft.

Space Station Work

Astronauts who live and work at the ISS have a variety of jobs. One of their tasks is to use sophisticated cameras to photograph the Earth. They often target specific regions, such as glaciers, coral reefs, and volcanoes. They also photograph cloud formations. Scientists can study these photographs to gain a better understanding of the planet. They can also learn more about climate change, and how human pollution affects different areas of the world.

John Phillips is an astronaut who traveled to the ISS in 2005. The United States was not operating space shuttles at that time, so Phillips traveled on a Russian spacecraft. As part of a NASA education program, Phillips installed a digital camera in the Earth-

Astronaut John Phillips works inside the International Space Station in 2005.

facing window. It was no ordinary camera, however —this one could be operated by remote control from Earth! More than 8,500 middle school students from all over the world took pictures with the camera. The pictures were then posted on the Internet. This project allowed students to photograph and examine the Earth just as if they were astronauts viewing the planet from space.

Every space mission is a team effort, and astronauts work closely together as a team. They all have their own responsibilities and jobs to do. Yet no matter what mission they are working on, or what projects they are assigned, every one of them plays a valuable role in the exploration of space.

CHAPTER 4

Meet an Astronaut

Many people have stories to tell about their jobs. They talk about what they do, people they know, and challenges they face. When Dr. Ellen Baker tells stories about her job, the things she says are especially fascinating. That is because she is an astronaut who has traveled into space on three different missions for NASA.

From Doctor to Astronaut

When Dr. Baker was a young girl, she loved all things related to space. Becoming an astronaut was not her goal, though. She explains why: "When I was growing up, I was fascinated by the early space flights—the Mercury and Gemini missions, and of course the exciting Apollo flights to the Moon. I was glued to my television set watching the coverage. But did I dream about going into space myself? No, because I grew up during the 1960s when becoming an astronaut was not yet an option for women."[9]

Dr. Baker decided to pursue a career in medicine. She finished college and medical school, and completed a three-year residency. Then she began to think about the possibility of working for NASA. "I had no idea that I would eventually be an astronaut," she says, "even though by that time

Mission specialist Dr. Ellen Baker performs a medical exam on a fellow astronaut during a shuttle mission.

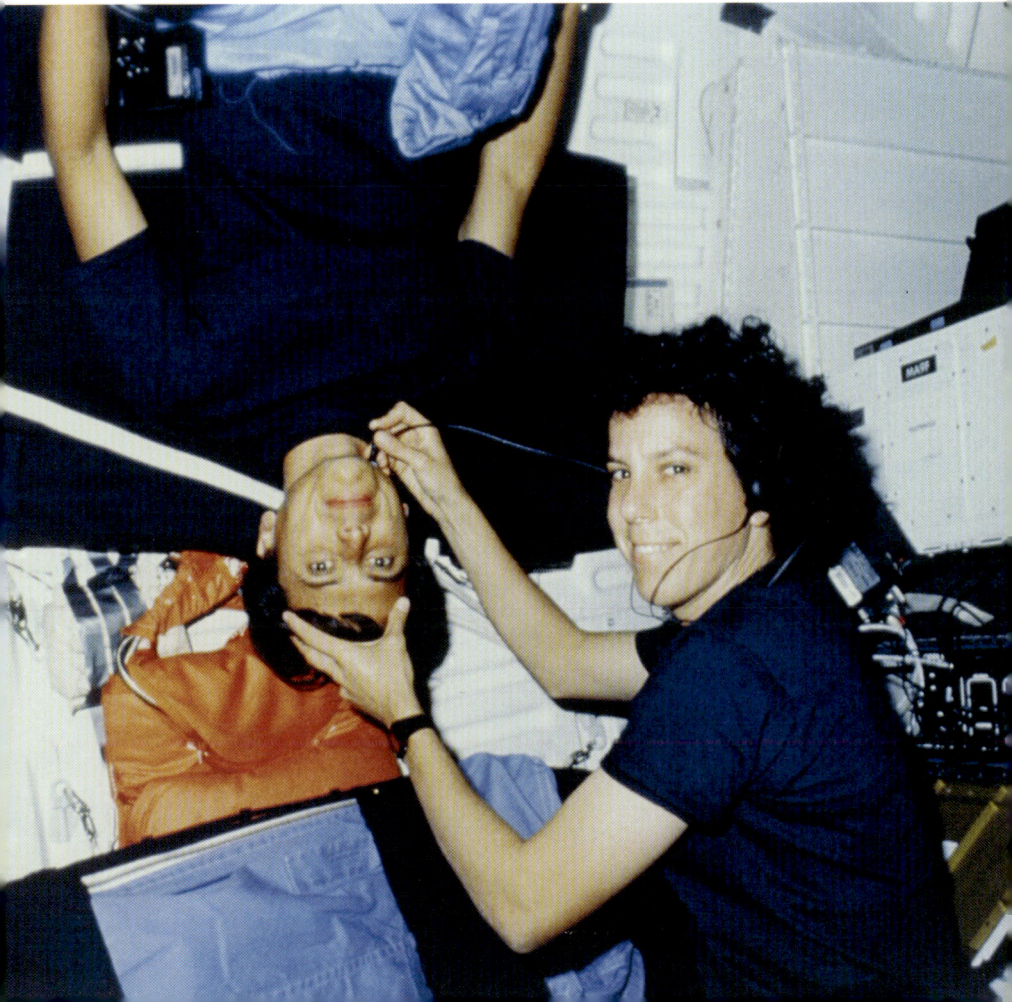

women were being accepted in the program. All I knew was that I wanted to be a part of NASA." In 1981, Dr. Baker was hired to be a medical officer at NASA's Johnson Space Center. She took care of astronauts and their families, and supported the early shuttle flights. After three years, she received some thrilling news—NASA had selected her to participate in the astronaut training program. "After being such an avid fan of the space program for all those years, I could hardly believe that I was going to be part of it. I would be able to visit space

Dr. Baker (second from left) and the crew of the space shuttle *Atlantis* pose for an in-flight photo. The 1989 mission was Dr. Baker's first trip into space.

just as astronauts before me had done. It is hard to explain the excitement I felt whenever I thought about it."

Space Missions

Four years later, after extensive training and preparation, Dr. Baker was chosen for a mission aboard the space shuttle *Atlantis*. She describes how she felt when the day of the launch arrived and the countdown started: "I had been to dozens of launches before in support of other flights, and had worked closely with the crews who flew on those missions. Plus, I had spent a lot of time in simulators, which are designed to make you think you're actually in space. So when I was up on the launchpad, it didn't seem all that different from just another training exercise. Then the countdown started and I heard those rockets fire, and the reality of what was happening hit me. I thought, 'Wow. This is really me up here, this is the real thing. I'm about to take off for space!'"

Dr. Baker says that after liftoff, the ride was rough at first but then things soon smoothed out. "As we were climbing through the atmosphere, all I could hear was the roar of the rockets and it was really loud. But just eight and half minutes into the flight, the main engines shut off and everything was quiet. There we were, just drifting along up there in space. It was incredible. But the real fun began when we unhooked our seatbelts and started

The crew of *Atlantis*, including Dr. Baker (top right), floats with the crew of the Russian space station *Mir* in 1995.

to float." Dr. Baker says she was surprised at how quickly she adjusted to being weightless. "I didn't suffer from the problems that some people have, such as feeling queasy or dizzy—although it is somewhat strange at first to find yourself and your fellow crew members floating sideways and upside down! But I got used to it pretty quickly, and soon I was very good at propelling myself along with my fingertips."

The mission lasted for five days. During that time, Dr. Baker and the *Atlantis* crew orbited the Earth 79 times and traveled 1.8 million miles (2.9 million km). One of their tasks was to carry along an unmanned spacecraft called *Galileo.* After the crew launched *Galileo,* it flew off to begin its own exploration of the planet Jupiter.

Dr. Baker flew on two more missions after that. In 1992, she was part of the crew on the space shuttle *Columbia.* Her third mission was in 1995, when she traveled again on *Atlantis.* That mission was historic because it was the first time the shuttle docked with the Russian space station Mir. When the two were linked together, they formed the largest spacecraft that had ever been in orbit. "It was very exciting to visit Mir and work with Russian cosmonauts," she says. "Although cosmonauts and astronauts grew up in very different

worlds, in space we worked well as a team and developed a lot of respect for each other. I think it would be exciting to spend several months aboard a space station, to really feel like you are living in space, rather than just visiting."

Gazing Down at Earth

When asked how it feels to look at the Earth from high above, Dr. Baker says, "In shuttle flights, you are only a few hundred miles above the Earth, but the view is just stunning. I could see natural features such as the oceans, rivers, volcanoes, and mountains. The man-made phenomena were beautiful as well. At night you can see cities all over the world with their lights twinkling in the black velvet sky." She adds that seeing the Earth from space can also be an emotional experience. "You develop this sense of attachment with places you see—you feel a bond to the Earth and to the people there. At times like that it is hard to imagine turmoil and strife when everything looks so pretty from above."

The Tough Times

Dr. Baker says she learned a long time ago that a certain amount of fear is just part of the job. "I think everybody has some anxiety and fear about going into space. It's dangerous—there's no question about that. Yet we are taught in our training to focus on the task that needs to be done, rather than focusing on danger or fear. That is necessary

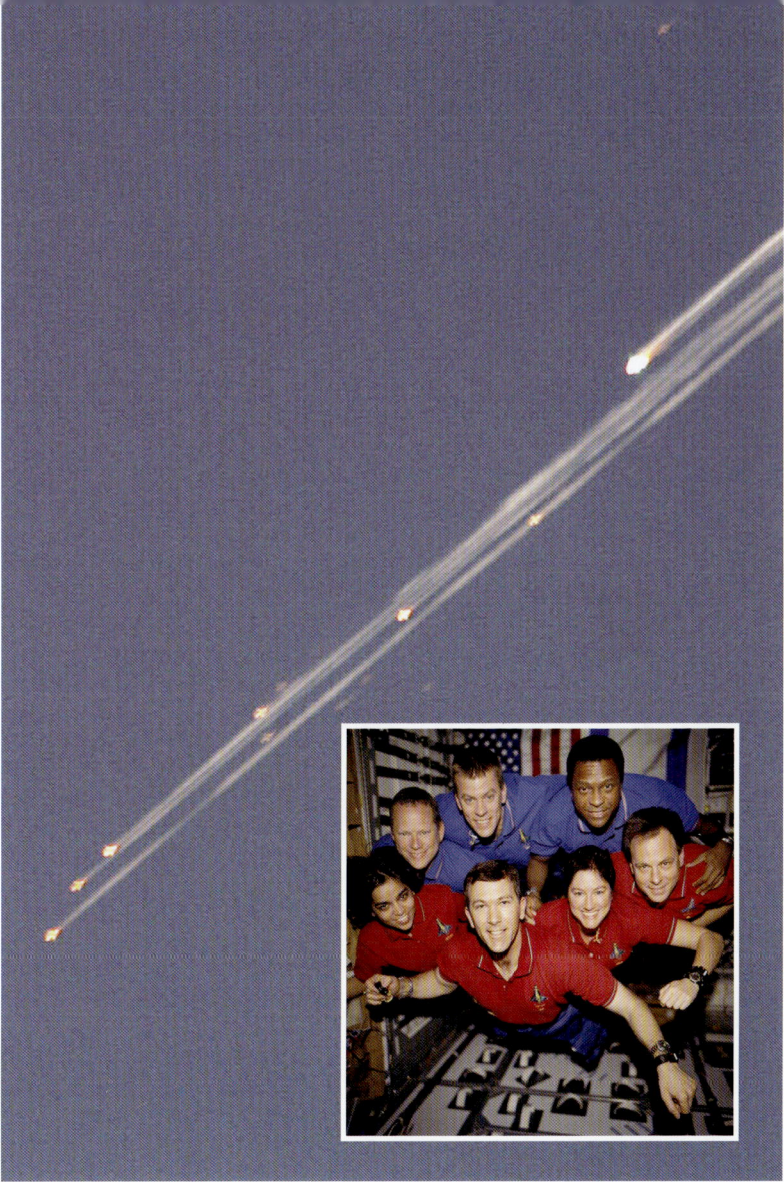

Debris from the space shuttle *Columbia* streaks through the sky in 2003. All seven crewmembers (inset) were killed in the disaster.

not only for astronauts, but also for police officers, firefighters, soldiers, or anyone else who works in risky professions. You can't let your anxiety get in the way of your performance or you'll be ineffective at your job. You just have to deal with it."

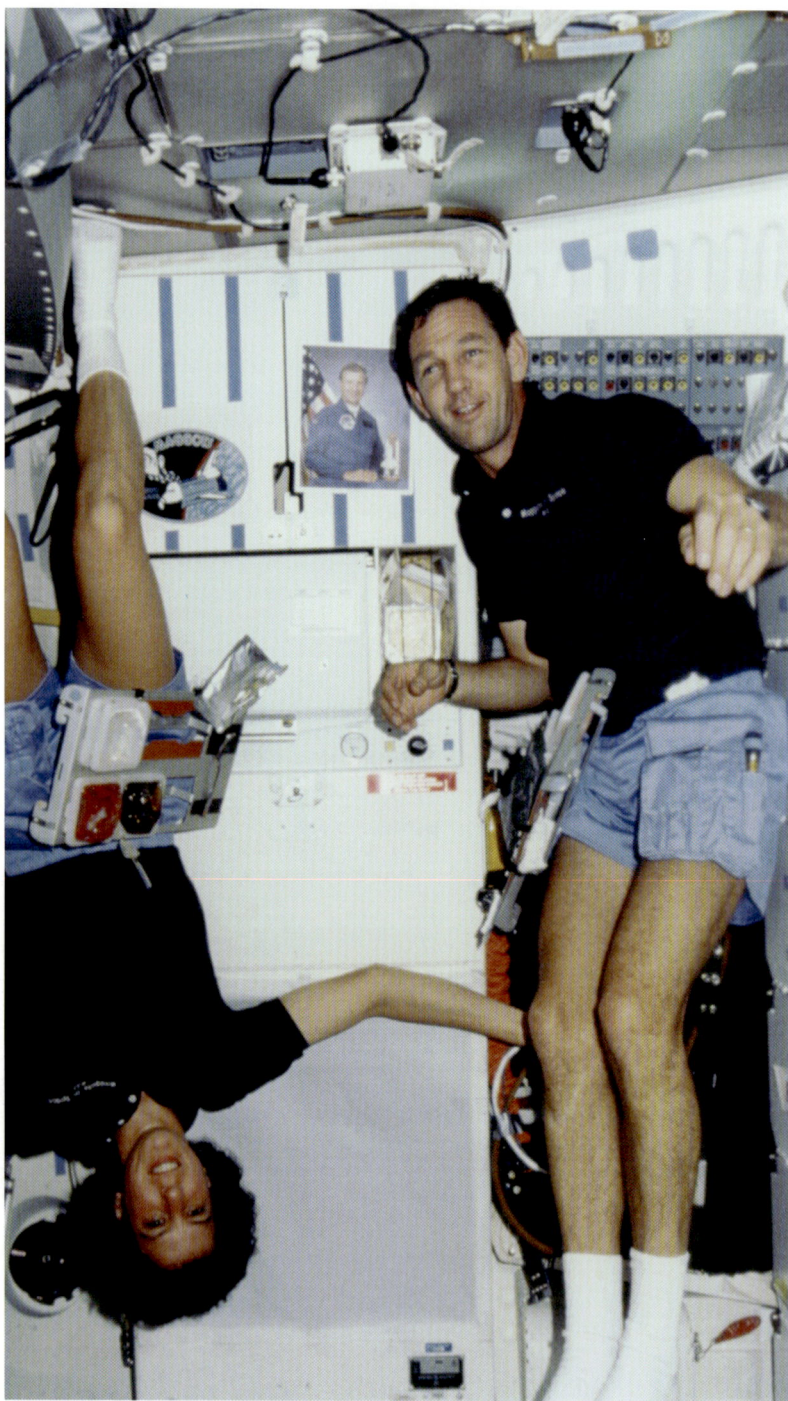

Dr. Baker and a colleague float inside *Atlantis* in 1989.

But there are times, she says, when it is impossible not to become emotional. "When the *Columbia* broke apart and we learned that all the astronauts were lost, it was one of the worst times for anyone working at NASA. The people on that spacecraft were our coworkers and our friends, and losing them was about as bad as it gets. . . . We're still not over it. And the truth is, we probably never will be over it. But we have to keep going. That's what they would want us to do."

Words of Wisdom

Dr. Baker says she has a message for young people who might dream of becoming astronauts. "Keep your focus on doing something you love, something you're passionate about, and give it everything you've got. No matter what you want to do in life, you have to work hard toward achieving your dream. If you want to be an astronaut, then make that your goal—but keep in mind that many, many people have the same dream you do, and it is highly competitive. If you pursue a career that you love, you'll be happy and fulfilled whatever you do. But if you are fortunate enough to become an astronaut, I can truthfully say there is no more wonderful career on Earth."

NOTES

Chapter 1: Star Sailors

1. Kathryn D. Sullivan, "The Ultimate Field Trip: An Astronaut's View of Earth," *Earth Observations and Imaging: A Journal of Human-Directed Remote Sensing from the Space Shuttle and International Space Station,* November 10, 2004. http://eol.jsc.nasa.gov/ newsletter/uft/uft1.htm.

Chapter 2: What It Takes To Be an Astronaut

2. Quoted in Kim Dismukes, "Preflight Interview: Eileen Collins," NASA Human Space Flight, February 22, 2005. http://spaceflight.nasa.gov/ shuttle/crew/intcollins.html.

3. Quoted in Liz Ruark, "Person of the Week: Pamela Melroy," Wellesley College, October 16, 2000. www.wellesley.edu/Anniversary/melroy. html.

4. Megan McArthur, interview with author, April 6, 2005.

5. McArthur, interview with author.

6. NASAexplores, "Pam Melroy." www.nasaexplores. com/extras/astronauts/melroy.html.

Chapter 3: Astronauts at Work

7. "Tom Jones: Astronaut," The Planetary Society. http://mmp.planetary.org/astro/jonet/jonet70.htm.
8. NASAexplores, "Docking with Precision," May 16, 2002. www.nasaexplores.com/show2_articlea. php?id=02-036.

Chapter 4: Meet an Astronaut

9. All quotes in chapter 4: Dr. Ellen S. Baker, interview with author, May 3, 2005.

GLOSSARY

booster rockets: Powerful rockets that propel a space shuttle away from Earth's atmosphere.

commander: The astronaut who is responsible for every aspect of a space mission.

cosmonauts: Astronauts from Russia.

dock: The process of linking two spacecraft together.

Hubble Space Telescope: A massive orbiting observatory that has been in space since 1990.

International Space Station (ISS): The world's largest space observatory in permanent orbit around the Earth.

mission specialists: Astronauts who carry out many tasks on space missions, such as conducting experiments, performing space walks, and maintaining and repairing equipment.

pilot: The astronaut who is second in command on a mission and who assists the commander in controlling and operating the spacecraft.

simulator: A device that mimics a real-life situation.

space shuttles: High-tech spacecraft that can blast off, complete a mission in space, and then fly back to Earth to be used again.

FOR FURTHER EXPLORATION

Books

James Buckley Jr., *Space Heroes: Amazing Astronauts.* New York: DK Publishing, 2004. The story of some of the world's greatest astronauts, including those who flew on the first Mercury space mission and others who have flown in space shuttles.

Simon Holland, *Space.* New York: DK Publishing, 2001. A colorful guide to astronomy for young readers, which features facts about space exploration, the solar system, planets, stars, and galaxies.

Bea Uusma Schyffert, *The Man Who Went to the Far Side of the Moon: The Story of Apollo 11 Astronaut Michael Collins.* San Francisco: Chronicle Books, 2003. This is a biography of astronaut Michael Collins, who was part of the crew of the first mission to land on the Moon.

Periodicals

Teri Cross, "The Lifeboat in Space," *Boys' Quest,* April/May 2004.

Annie Schleicher, "NASA Prepares for Shuttle Launch," *NewsHour Extra,* April 21, 2005.

Hugh Westrup, "Flights of Fancy? Did NASA Fake

Its Missions to the Moon?" *Current Science,* March 5, 2004.

Internet Source

Nancy Finton, "Living It Up in Space," *National Geographic Explorer,* October 2001. http://magma. nationalgeographic.com/ngexplorer/0110/articles/ iss_0110.html.

Web Sites

How Stuff Works, Space Channel (www.how stuffworks.com/space_channel.htm). Includes a variety of informative articles about becoming an astronaut, as well as information about space shuttles, space stations, and weightlessness.

NASA Educator Astronaut Program (http://ed space.nasa.gov). An excellent resource with helpful information about astronaut careers, the jobs astronauts do, and virtual training exercises young people can do to see if they are cut out to be astronauts.

NASAexplores (www.nasaexplores.com). An excellent site for aspiring astronauts that includes numerous articles about space flight, astronaut profiles, glossaries, and a "Just for Fun" section with activities and games.

NASA's Kids' Science News Network (http:// ksnn.larc.nasa.gov). This entertaining site uses animation and video to introduce science, technology, engineering, and mathematics concepts to young people.

INDEX

PICTURE CREDITS

ABOUT THE AUTHOR

Peggy J. Parks holds a bachelor of science degree from Aquinas College in Grand Rapids, Michigan, where she graduated magna cum laude. An avid fan of science and astronomy, Parks has written more than forty titles for Thomson Gale's KidHaven Press, Blackbirch Press, and Lucent Books. She lives in Muskegon, Michigan, a town she says inspires her writing because of its location on the shores of Lake Michigan.